Charles Ingersoll

A Letter to a Friend in a Slave State

Charles Ingersoll

A Letter to a Friend in a Slave State

ISBN/EAN: 9783744732390

Printed in Europe, USA, Canada, Australia, Japan

Cover: Foto ©ninafisch / pixelio.de

More available books at **www.hansebooks.com**

A LETTER

TO A FRIEND IN A SLAVE STATE.

BY A

CITIZEN OF PENNSYLVANIA.

PHILADELPHIA.
1862.

LETTER TO A FRIEND IN A SLAVE STATE.

My dear——

EVERYBODY recollects the turn given to the idea that the fence of the law cannot be made perfect, when the Englishman said he never saw an Act of Parliament he could not drive his coach through ; now signalized, alas ! but a thousand years too soon, in the illustrious instance of the Constitution of the United States. Any one or more of the States which drove into this great work may drive out again by the Southern road, and we are taught by lessons, both Legislative and Executive, that as long as the States which remain to us are united, the Constitution is unwounded, though the Northern chariot and scythes be driven through every clause of it. What the South accomplishes at a blow, we do piecemeal. Eight millions of people hold that, if a State had called a convention and asked of the Federal Government a boon, which was refused, or being refused nothing whatever, had expressed a preference to live alone, they might make their act of constitutional secession, and bow themselves out of the Union. Nor would it be possible to exaggerate the heresies of those that are leading the fortunes of the other eighteen millions, who assail, in his liberty and property, the plainest rights of the citizen ; who mean to consolidate the Government, if they can, and whose schemes for the consolidation of large parts of it, are already before Congress. These are the extremes of thought and action that accompany national calamity.

1

In any other part of the globe the next act would be anarchy, the edifice would come down and crush its inhabitants under the ruins of centuries ; but our house was built yesterday, with our own hands, and we can hold it up if we will. We must not deceive ourselves; we must accept, what is upon us, as revolution. If we conquer the South and take possession of their vanquished country, it is revolution; to make peace and separate from them, for which there is no power in the Constitution, would be revolution, and that revolution is the name that applies to our existing condition, every man's senses assure him.

We are in the midst of civil war, to North and South alike unexpectedly ; for when was civil war deliberated on ? The North did not believe the South would leave them ; the South did not believe the North would fight to retain them ; the South armed and struck the blow, and now the sword is drawn on both sides, and cannot be sheathed without conquest or a compromise. We have to conquer the South or settle with them; and their unconditional conquest seems the policy of those that rule us.

The purpose of this letter is to explain to you some of the views of the persons in this State who regard conciliation as our only available resort, and look upon the extreme course of the Government as ruin.

In such a crisis, the most perilous in which a nation can stand, of what materials is composed the party in possession of the Government, and which controls our destinies? They may be classed under three heads. The original abolitionists who engage themselves, without disguise or denial, in the work for which they where ordained, and which they have from the beginning, when they were but a speck on the remote horizon, steadily pursued, that of destroying the Constitution and Union; the political abolitionists, or those who, for the sake of power and access to the treasury, have adopted their principles, and act with them ; and last, the body of the Republicans, who voted for

Mr. Lincoln as the anti-Democratic candidate, and who, sincerely attached to both the Constitution and the Union, yet stand helplessly by, and allow the stakes of national existence to be played by the abolitionists.

If the President and his advisers were reliable men, though the philosophy of freedom teaches to distrust power, every citizen with the love of country in his breast, would be disposed, in a great emergency, to bestow on them a liberal confidence ; but when his want of force and their want of virtue are the vice of our position, instead of the call not to embarrass the Government, which we hear from so many mouths when a measure of the administration is challenged, a watchful jealousy is the duty of all.

Nothing but a restoration of the Union can save us. Peace and a separation cannot be agreed on with the South ; the President and Senate having no power to make a treaty by which the Union is divided. It would have the effect of restoring the States, upon the instant, to the condition of independent sovereignty, in which they stood before they came under the Constitution of 1789. And the attempt which you may expect to see, some day, made by Mr. Lincoln's government, to give effect to the secession of at least part of the South, by letting them go, would be futile. The President and Senate may enter into treaties with foreign nations, but they cannot convert into foreign nations, States of the Union. What then is to become of us ?

Mr. Seward has well said that we are not to break at what he calls a " *line of latitude* ;" meaning probably that the present line, between the two hostile sections of the country, or any other line, could never be a permanent demarcation of boundaries. When he stated his proposition, he struck a chord which vibrates to every heart, for the question directly follows, if we cannot divide by this line, and if the States cannot live isolated in their separate sovereignties, and it is plain they could not, what line is there to divide by ; and if, which is equally plain, there is none, where shall we be, and where find habitation for our liberties, when the Union is broken up ? When we came together in 1790, we had never been separated ; we had not quarrelled ; yet the Union was effected with much difficulty, and not at the first intention ; though having all the advantage of the auspices of Washington and the other men of that day.

If, by some process of disintegration, through political mishap, the territory of any people, for example, France—a very compact country, which has added to its square miles from century to century—could be divided by a "line of latitude," or separated into the many parts which originally composed it, so that those, which once were independent sovereignties, might live alone, and those which were wrested from Germany, Spain and England, renew their relations with them, it is plain that these disjointed members, if they did not come together again as France, would have altogether new combinations to form. Now in what particular would our condition, in case of final disunion, whether divided into two parts or many, be better than theirs?

We have existence as an united country, by compact, a fairer and better than any other that could be devised, and which was for seventy-one years respected. If it be broken, not to be renewed, our condition is just as much worse than would be that of France, as the cohesion of the provinces of a country, accustomed to highly centralized rule, is greater than that of a system of States in a union or confederacy. Where then, the force of arms and habit that united France, the force of compact that united us, being broken, would be found the new combinations that must settle their destinies ? The answer is, *in war!* War gave to France, in about a thousand years of fighting and negotiating, their territory as we see it to-day. This process must be with them begun, for the second time, and

with us, for the first. Every cause of strife, that makes war
so frequent between the different powers of the earth, that
it may be said to be always imminent, would be reason
enough for hostilities among us; and there would be ele-
mental questions to settle besides.

In Europe their map is made. Each country has its
identity, any two or more of them may engage in conflict;
but it would not be allowed to affect a question which has
been settled for them, for centuries, and must not be touched,
not only because it has long since been decided, but because
it is the interest of other nations, of that part of the world,
for the sake of the general peace to insist upon, and, if need
be, enforce it. To alter the map of Europe by the annexation of a part of Savoy to the French Empire, though by
treaty between the nations concerned, backed with the consent of the population affected, as expressed by their votes
at the polls, startled the Continent.

But what map have we, when there is no longer the
United States of America? There is no identity for Pennsylvania or any other State, when the Union is broken up.
They are not nations, founded, fixed and established, but
things of yesterday, whose relations with themselves and
with surrounding territory, were based upon, and adjusted
to the Union; which being gone, there is no indentity left
to be respected, and if there were, no power to enforce it.
War, therefore, would be with us a necessity of our situa-
tion, and not as with other countries, an occasional fact, de-
pending on accident, interest or passion. It would be our
normal condition until we came to a settlement; and that
could only be when we had mastered one another. Whoever will look at our present map will perceive that the
states are devided, for the most part, by surveyors' lines.
Pennsylvania, which bounds on six States, Delaware, Maryland, Virginia, Ohio, New York, and New Jersey, is separated from five of them by the surveyor, and from one
only by a natural boundary, so that, perchance, the farmer

in plowing his field, does not know whether he is plowing
Pennsylvania or Virginia. When we had the Union, this
was cement to it; but make us no longer one, and it becomes the source of bitter and incessant hostilities.

We must be broken and shaped into nations; the process
will be long, and nobody can anticipate its results. The
strong will establish themselves behind rivers, chains of
mountains, and lines of fortresses, and encroaching on the
weak, annex, absorb and divide them into provinces, or rule
and scourge them as colonies. States will recede or advance—some will become great nations, others will disap-
pear, and new ones will arise, as Poland has left the family
of nations, and Holland and Prussia have come into it; as
France and Russia have advanced, and Austria and Swe-
den receded. South Carolina, with her swamps and rice
fields, will fall a prey to the more vigorous regions of
the upper country of Georgia and Tennessee. Ohio,
Virginia and Kentucky, which, on their fertile soils
could maintain four hundred souls to the square mile, will
be strong: New England, which could not support a third
of that number, will be weak; and so must be immense
tracts of country in the South which are better adapted to
the mosquito and crocodile than to the habitation of man.
Physical force, measured by population, and the number of
men they can bring into the field, will settle all mooted
points, and neither South Carolina nor Massachusetts, which
will have had so much hand in doing away with the old
form of abitrament, would find reason to congratulate
themselves on the new.

In the midst of these discords, and it would be long before the questions dividing the country were sufficiently settled to give hostilities any other character than that of civil
war, liberty would be engulphed. We see now, in the first
stage of our disturbances, the proneness of power to usur-
pation and violence; we witness audacities which, a year
ago, would have been pronounced impossible. Already the

liberties of the citizen are a thing not jealously regarded ; and we are told that the Government must be sustained to-day, and the Constitution righted to-morrow. But for this fatal mistake of our rights, and of the duty we owe our country, and the yet more flagrant error that it is not in the power of events to do us permanent political injury, under the influence of which we made our first mis-step, and by which we seem to this day to be infatuated, we would not be where we are.

That this is not only an unexaggerated, but the only view to be taken of our future, in the event of failure to restore the Union, and dividing at a "line of latitude," or in any other manner, we learn by lessons taught in the history of the world, on too many of its pages, to be doubted either by the exalted, like Mr. Seward, or the more humble, like you and me. We might swear to treaties and enter into well-schemed divisions of the country ; and they might last a few feverish years, but the sword must make our map at last.

A word now—the question for the country being war or compromise—upon the war which we are at this time waging, and the probabilities, as they strike people generally, of its success as a war of conquest. Let us suppose to ourselves all the advantages of an immense force. Let us grant we can keep it up to 700,000 men, and that is out of the question, for no free people will pay heavy taxes, which in the much burdened countries are imposed by one class, and paid by another, and not imposed by the people on themselves. Let us also suppose, which is equally out of the question, that for any length of time we can safely tempt authority with the control of such a force.

You and I would not venture to criticise campaigns, but there are things belonging to them, as plain to the common soldier as to the commander-in-chief. If we had declared war with England, or taken the chances of one, rather than pass under the Caudine forks and surrender Mason and Slidell, the people might have praised the firmness of their rulers; but if pursuing the bold train of his diplomatic thinking, when just before, Mr. Seward expressed himself to his representatives abroad, as ready to fight all Europe together, should they cross his path,* he had gone to war, not to save our honor, but with the object of conquering and keeping the British islands, we should, any of us, have been able to give good reasons against so extreme an undertaking.

We must assume that the South will resist with all their might, and that our progress in their territory is to be effected by force of arms. Not only has there been no evidence, but the contrary, by many Northern witnesses, of a desire to see a Northern army among them; and whatever the Union feeling in the South, if kindly dealt with, it is against all reason and probability that a spirited and free people should invite to their conquest a government, however legitimate, which their immediate State, by organized action, and a majority of their people, has agreed to throw off. It is in the nature of men, especially freemen, to be regulated by the will of the majority, a human instinct on which republican government is founded, which carried us through the Revolution of '76, when a minority submitted their opinions, and which we see operate in the daily circumstances of life, where the leading few commonly infuse their ideas into and

---

* See at page 200 of the volume of notes and despatches lately published by the Department of State—Mr. Seward's despatch to Mr. Dayton, 22nd of April, 1861: "Not entertaining the least apprehension of the departure from that course by his Majesty's Government, it is not without some reluctance that the President consents to the suggestion of some considerations affecting France herself, which you may urge in support of it. * * * Foreign intervention would oblige us to treat those who should yield it as allies of the insurrectionary party, and to carry on the war against them as enemies. The case would not be relieved, but, on the contrary, would only be aggravated, if several European States should combine in that intervention. The President and the people of the United States deem the Union, which would then be at stake, worth all the cost and all the sacrifices of a contest with the world in arms, if such a contest should prove inevitable."

control the action of the many. We also assume that the troops of either side fight equally well, with the single difference that the South has the advantage of us in contending in defence of their homes. As to the claim of superior skill on the part of Southern generals, it seems to be not only against probabilities, but disproved by facts. We further assume that we fight with, not on our part prodigiously superior numbers, for, though we are much the more numerous population, and able to pay more soldiers, yet, having to invade a widely extended territory, there is no reason why they should not be as strong as we are, at the point of conflict.

If then the forces are of nearly equal numbers, and equally well led, how ought we to count the chances, the question being the conquest of the Southern States ? In Missouri, Kentucky and other states, where, divided in opinion, they resist the secession movement, Northern armies find a country in which, no more being necessary than to give military aid to the well-affected part of the population, conquest is not in question : but the vast region comprising Western Tennessee, Arkansas, Louisiana, Texas, Florida, Alabama, Mississippi, Georgia, South Carolina, North Carolina, and Eastern Virginia, have to be brought to submission by the sword. I do not mean, by the sword, the sort of ruin like that of the iron pot coming against the earthen one—which must ensue to them at last, as co-terminous neighbors of a hostile people, stouter, stronger, richer and more numerous than themselves—but military subjugation. To accomplish this, to invade, conquer and occupy, it is indispensable that our military movements have the positiveness and certainty of those of trained armies, led by experienced officers, and supported by a vigorous government, supplying them with constant reinforcements.

We begin, subject to the immense disadvantage of being without the necessary foundation on which to build ; for the handful of soldiers who composed the army before these

2

troubles came on us, cannot serve as a frame for a force of 718,000 men. It is the best military opinion that the French revolution could not, for want of soldiers, have conquered its way, and must have broken down, notwithstanding the rush of the people into the ranks from all classes, had it not been for the remains of the old royal army, which the republicans used as the basis for their new military establishment. If, having an organized army of 359,000 disciplined men, we add to it 359,000 more, making up our number of 718,000, it is plain that the whole establishment would be alike in its parts when the recruits had had a few months of drill and discipline, every ten of them being alongside of ten soldiers, whose experience and knowledge would instruct them and inspire them with confidence; but if the whole 718,000 be equally raw and ignorant, they can be educated only by marching and fighting, and must for their primary instruction go through, in the field, a course of reverses and successes. We are now at the second stage of our education, that of successes, on a very long course of schooling that is before us. As to officers, beginning with almost none, which, considering our immense force, may be said to be the case, our condition must needs be much worse than in the department of soldiers.

The invaded South might lose twenty battles and not be conquered, while the loss of one by the invading North, when their work was almost accomplished, might be fatal, and operations to be begun again from the beginning. In 1808, the finest troops in the world were in possession of a great part of Spain, when the battle of Baylen lost them every foot of it but that which was north of the river Ebro, and on the confines of their own country.

Have we then an invading force? one with which to conquer, take and keep military possession? War is a trade, and armies only a machine. Our soldiers are brave, but courage, as was said by one who must have known, is not the first quality of a soldier. The question is, do they, taken together, make that machine so difficult to adjust, a disciplined army—are they a force which can be carried to the field, and relied on to struggle with the realities of war—cold, hunger, fatigue and privation, the miseries of the roadside and the hospital, without becoming disorganized; not merely, though that is not easy, when engaged with the enemy, to advance with alacrity and retire in good order?

The events of the memorable day of Bull Run, answer this question. We may have some better soldiers than then we had; men who have been under fire and done their duty well; but the character of our force must be the same, new levies led by new officers.

It would seem, taking the Southern accounts with our own that from about 10 o'clock, when the engagement began, to between 3 and 4 in the afternoon, when it ended in a panic rout, we constantly gained ground and lost none, and finally took flight, simply and merely because we were not soldiers enough to make a retreat in the presence of the enemy, when owing to his being reinforced or from some other cause not perfectly agreed on, by both sides, a backward movement had become necessary. Armies have been seized with panic before the 21st of July, 1861. This has happened so often that we were able to console ourselves, in our disgrace, with instances of it from all countries; but the fact, for it was without necessity, and for no reason in the world than because we did not know how to retire, went to prove, and did prove, that our soldiers were unsure.

But if good troops everywhere have been sometimes panic-struck, good troops nowhere ever acted such a part as did the Southern army when ours fled before it. Their enemy flying, in the last confusion, had scattered themselves, and left, unprotected and uncovered, the capital of their country, distant thirty-four miles, one day's forced march; and that place, for a certain number of days, if not weeks, they had only to enter and possess, if they had had troops with which, abandoning their position, and the forests and fastnesses under cover of which they fought, they could have ventured the simplest operation in the open field, without incurring the hazard, in their turn, of military disaster. But far from advancing on the place thus lying at their discretion, they did not, in any force, so much as pursue, and the foe was allowed, while they must have had under their hands a very large army, of which any 10,000 men capable of being moved, might have entered Washington, to collect again his disbanded forces, repair his losses, restore his condition, then lie for months opposite them, stronger than he was the day before the defeat took place, and finally to see them retire.

Any general, they say, may gain a battle, for it may be given him by his adversary; the true general is he that can reap the fruits of success; but no want of generalship would explain this most remarkable forbearance, which could be accounted for by nothing but the want of solidity of their soldiers. All kinds of reasons have been suggested for it: a defensive policy, bad weather, imperfect information, ignorance of the extent of their success, that they did not want the seat of government of the United States, with others equally unsatisfactory. If they were all founded in truth, and were combined together, it is not imaginable that that army would not have been in Washington, if they could have been taken there. When General Ross seized Washington, he did not hold it forty-eight hours; but the political as well as the military effect of its fall was immense. When Wellington, the most cautious of commanders, and not a man to give the substance for the shadow, had the choice, after his victory of Salamanca, to pursue, with the hope of destroying the enemy, or take, and immediately abandon Madrid, at the hazard of being overwhelmed by three armies, then in the field against him, he marched on the capital, although he knew he could not remain there, and, in fact, came within an ace of being cut off, in retiring from it.

The capture of Washington, beside its prodigious military results, would have had such an echo everywhere, both here and in Europe, where it would have been worth to them, probably, the recognition they so much covet, that, granting no more than rationality to the Southern leaders, its remaining in our hands after the day at Bull Run, can be accounted for in one way only. It is altogether incredible that they were so unworthy of their trust, as immediately upon such a success, to remain ignorant for days of the state of things, just on their front, or that they were reluctant to rouse Maryland behind us, or that their defensive policy would be interfered with by seizing the enemy's capital, lying before them, any more than his camp equipage or artillery, that he left behind him. The simple truth is, General Beauregard's troops could not be relied upon; he may explain his course in after-dinner speeches, and quote Alcibiades till doomsday,

"Audacious drink, and greatly daring dine,"

but turn it as he will, in his carousals in celebration of that not unprecedented event in war, a defeat without a victory, it could have been alone the discretion which is the better part of valor, which, begetting diffidence of the materials of his army, made him forbear to snatch so great a prize.*

Here, then, was an army, composed of materials as good as ours, longer than we had been under military organization and discipline, which had defended themselves well in their position, not only wholly unable to invade, as we must, an enemy's country on a long line of operations, but

---

* Since the text was written, General Beauregard's official report has been added to his speech, and published in the North. It may be taken for absolute proof, inferring from what he says, and does not say, because not "proper to be * * * communicated," of what could not be doubted before.

unwilling to hazard, in the flush of success, a march of thirty-four miles, in the open field, to reach his Capital. How long must it be before an army of such soldiers and such officers could be depended on to make their way through the North to the line of Canada? If the contending parties could have changed places, and we had been attacked behind cover, and they our assailants, we should have had the victory, and they have undergone the defeat; when they could make no impression on us, instead of retreating, they would have fled in disorder, and we, in our turn, would have been unable to move and gather the harvest of success.

When we march our soldiers against those of the South, while theirs do exactly the work to which they are competent—that of making good in the midst of a friendly population, a region fortified by nature with deep ravines, broad rivers, high hills, narrow passes, and the never-ending forest;—we, on the contrary, have to take the open field, and there contend with obstacles at every step. The best troops, in a position fortified by nature or art, and assailed by troops only equally good, may by valor and pertinacity of assault, be overcome : but let both armies be composed of raw soldiers, and the troops behind cover fight well, while those who have to make an assault requiring vigor and determination, cannot be depended on. Jackson, entrenched at New Orleans, with a very imperfect force, successfully resisted excellent troops, but, after having cut them to pieces, he allowed them, though a man all fire and action, to retreat unmolested, because he did not deem it safe to move against them in the field. The attacking army at Waterloo, to take another familiar illustration, veterans playing desperately their last stake, under a consummate commander, were very superior to the defending army, composed of soldiers of different nations, hastily brought together, and some of them so lately on the other side, that they were yet in their French uniforms; but the position made the difference, and they fought without decisive advantage until the party assailed was reinforced. Had the assailants been raw soldiers, and had the defences they attacked, instead of being intrenchments, farm buildings and unevennesses of the ground, been such prodigious works as are everywhere established by nature among us, they would have had no possible chance. When General Braddock, with a regular force, undertook to penetrate the American forest, his army was destroyed by a handful of French soldiers, with a few Canadian militia and Indians.

But a glance at a map, showing the area of the Southern States, which is much greater than that of the territory of any European power, except Russia, the State of Texas alone being as large as France, or Spain and Portugal, will satisfy us that the South have an ally that is altogether invincible, in *space*. Space, when the scale is great, is, in a war of invasion, too much for any military power that can be brought against it. It had well nigh conquered Napoleon in Russia, who was exhausted in contending with it before he was attacked by the frost and snow. We invaded Canada three several times during the war of 1812, in considerable force, and with the fullest confidence of overrunning the country, but were, each time, quite unable to make any impression on that extended region, defended though it was by but few British troops. Alexander the Great covered space more vast than that which is before our armies, inhabited, however, for the most part, by effeminate nations, but neither Julius Cæsar nor Napoleon ever performed such a feat, and, if they could be brought to Washington to advise with Mr. Lincoln, would assure him it was not possible. To keep the line open, if that were all, would be a military marvel; and what would communication be, and transportation, costing as they do now, when we came to reach the Rio Grande?

As to detached expeditions against the coast, which serve

to annoy and distress an enemy, but, however gallantly conducted, not to carry us into the country, they exasperate the population against which they are directed, without advancing us an inch beyond the ground we occupy; of which the numerous English expeditions to our own shores and those of Europe are signal proof. If we detach 15,000 men against a given point of the Southern coast, the 15,000 put there by the enemy to defend it, have infinitely the advantage of them, for they are in their own country, and within reach of everything, while we can only communicate with our supplies and reinforcements, at great loss of time, and the largest expenditure of money. We must be able to possess ourselves of not merely Charleston, Norfolk, New Orleans, and Savannah, but the whole country to which they belong; and establishing ourselves at these places, however important, would give us only a foothold from which to make our progress.

What progress in the conquest of North and South Carolina have we made from Beaufort, from Hatteras, from Roanoke, and in the conquest of Tennessee from Nashville? How much would be furthered the work if we occupied Richmond? If the Southern troops were withdrawn from Virginia, North Carolina and Tennessee to the country south of them, leaving us to operate against the cotton States, across a hostile and desolated region, or from the coast, we should only be where we were before hostilities began.

North Carolina and Tennessee were of the Southern States, two of the truest to the Union; North Carolina always the antipodes of South Carolina, and Tennessee by climate, soil and population, more western than southern, and through the powerful and long-exercised influence of General Jackson, strongly prejudiced against the doctrines of Mr. Calhoun. And now, having occupied the capital of Tennessee, and Newbern and other places on the shores of North Carolina, what have we done towards bringing back those States? If their Union feeling is not to be stirred by the sound of the Northern drum, of which, probably, we are satisfied, we have to bring them back, and then to control them, by arms. Has such a task been begun? Do you expect to see it attempted? Are we to believe it ever will be? And if we are not to think of military reduction of the people, and if they do not voluntarily flock to our standard, are not, to-day, North Carolina and Tennessee further from the Union than before we marched troops on them; infinitely further in Union feeling, and not nearer, militarily?

If, after their success at Bull Run, the South had not only seized Washington, but pushing forward, been able to hoist the Secession colors over the towns along the southern boundary of Pennsylvania,—Philadelphia, Lancaster, York, Gettysburg, Pittsburg, and the rest—is it to be inferred that the people of this State would be coming forward, to swear allegiance to the South; or, that before they could be induced to organize a Secession government, pay Secession taxes, send Senators and Members to the Secession Congress, and join the Southern Confederacy, the entire State must not be thoroughly reduced by the power of arms? Would seizing those places have given them possession of Pennsylvania? Would their armies, in holding them, have brought more of our territory under the influence of Mr. Jefferson Davis, than exactly that portion of it which was within their lines? Let those who throw up their hats and cry, the war is over, or that the beginning of the end has arrived, in this or that Southern State, because we have made a lodgment there, ask themselves, taking one reflecting moment to it, what the operation is, by which, and by which alone, the military reduction of a country can be effected, and they will see the emptiness, idleness, and vanity of such a thought.

If having armies on their soil, be not a commencement of the systematic work of military subjugation, how long we can remain at points remote from supply and reinforcement,

3

and what measures of soldierly severity may be, in the meantime, required to keep down discontent and insurrection on the part of the inhabitants, are questions that military men must answer; as the Medical Staff must inform us of the chances of life in the case of northern constitutions, exposed and tried like those of the soldier, in such climates as are found in portions of the southern country, after the hot season begins.

Of what avail would it be, could we navigate, in our gunboats, every stream from the mighty Mississippi to the shallowest of them, if we did not conquer and take military possession of the country which they water? We have been now at war twelve months, and with the best materials for an army, to be found in the world—a free people, accustomed to the use of fire-arms—what have we accomplished? In the hostile country, (I do not speak of semifriendly countries, like Maryland, Kentucky, and Missouri, which, before the fighting began, were wholly friendly.) we are at certain points on the coast, carried thither by the navy; we are at Nashville, *via*, partly, the Cumberland river, and have just begun to penetrate Eastern Virginia; but we have nowhere penetrated, with our bayonets, to the promised stratum of Union feeling; and we have everywhere raised against ourselves, in the bosom of the whole invaded population, a feeling of detestation, which, when they can no longer defend them, exhibits itself in burning their houses, crops, towns and villages, before our advancing colors, and in some instances, leaving poison behind them, as they fled, in the wells, and in the food which our troops were to consume; a feeling of deep hate, which no invading army, in any part of the world, ever failed to arouse: for an army is, at best, a terror to the fields and cities it pours its flood over; and which, new soldiers, like ours, of all others, must needs produce in the most frightful abundance. The South are discouraged, no doubt of it; they ought to be; the reality is upon them; they will be unable, unless aided from abroad, to fight us in the doubtful States, and must restrict their operations to territory absolutely their own, where secession is undiluted; and there the tide of battle will roll, with various success, sometimes with us, sometimes with them, but always in brothers' blood, until both parties, disgusted and shocked by the unnatural controversy, become satisfied, at last, of the truth of what Bishop Berkeley said, that it is not individuals alone, but nations sometimes, that go mad.

Did you ever hear of a *people* that were conquered? In the great wars of the beginning of the present century, kingdoms where overrun, and peace dictated in the capitals of half dethroned monarchs; but the people made no resistance; it was only to overcome the army; and when it came, in Spain, and to some degree in Russia, to conquering also the inhabitants of the country, military power seemed to be dealing with air or water, on which no lasting impression could be made. Poland was seized ninety years ago, and partitioned by three adjacent neighbors, among them, at that and subsequent periods, so greatly their superiors in strength, that no war for conquest, when the country was entered, took place; but, at this day, if we are to believe the newspapers, the people in parts of Poland are in a state of insurrection. The north of Italy was, during some ten centuries, almost constantly under foreign occupation, so powerful as to be overwhelming; but the people where not changed into Germans, Frenchmen, or Spaniards, when they sate on their necks in turn; they remained Italians, always discontented and revolting, and now seem, with the aid of foreign intervention, to have thrown off the yoke at last. Do we entertain of our own blood so poor an opinion, as for a moment to suppose we could ever beat into the Union the people of the South?

The great powers of Europe are constantly fighting, but how often do they make a conquest of one another, in Mr Lincoln's sense of taking, holding and keeping? Although it is to be observed that in a war for conquest, they would have the great advantage over us, of operating, not only with long organized armies, supplied with all the material of scientific war, but also in territory, dotted at every strategical point, with fortified places and strongholds, by means of which, when the conquest is made, the country can be held; while our armies, on the contrary, in this, so lately happy and peaceful land of ours, if the South were conquered, would have to keep it, not with soldiers at Dantzics and Magdeburgs, but lying in the fields and open towns. If the Southern country were handed over to us to-day, and we were permitted to put down so many men here, and so many there, at points selected for the purpose, by military skill, how long could we hold it?

When the Cabinet say to an officer, there is the enemy, take an army and operate against him, he obeys, whatever he may think of the chances of success; but that is not enough for the country, whose all is at stake. When the Government shall tell us that a military scheme has been submitted, not for a movement, which may prove useful, on the Potomac, the Cumberland, or the Mississippi, which, or any other such, can be made for the South, as well as for the North, and can only be a victory, more or less serving to keep up the price of public securities, and float the Administration for a certain number of days; but a comprehensive plan for the general subjugation of the Southern States, despite all opposition of the population of that part of the country, then, and not till then, the people of the North will begin to think possible, what they now deem out of the question.

We may not be right, we people of Pennsylvania, who have seen no enemy since Sir William Howe left us; but these are our opinions of the war now waging against our brethren of the South.

And if we be wrong, are not compromise and conciliation better than war? We have, among the powers of the world, one friend, the great head of the Russian Empire: and in the late note of his Minister of Foreign Affairs to the Representative of the Government of the Czar at Washington, on the Mason and Slidell difficulty, he is told to reiterate to the President " the assurance of * * * the satisfaction " with which his Imperial Majesty would see the American " Union consolidated by measures of CONCILIATION."

Why should not the strong conciliate ; why should not the head of an army of seven hundred and eighteen thousand men compromise ? Whoever, let him be the most passionate Repubican of them all, will recollect what always has been, and now is the way of the world, must admit that compromise is not a policy, but a necessity. In religion, what we call toleration, which is compromise, has become the rule of Christendom ; the opposite system being abandoned. If the Emperor of Germany had compromised with the Protestant influence, his successor, this day, would be the arbiter of Europe; but he preferred war, and after thirty years' fighting had to come to compromise at last, with a loss of power which never has been, or can be recovered. George III. was an uncompromising monarch, and lost his thirteen colonies. James II., in the same way, lost his crown. Wellington was called the Iron Duke, but he was a man of eminent good sense, and he compromised with the Catholics rather than quarrel with them. The first Napoleon ruined himself by an uncompomrising foreign policy; but his papers, now in course of publication by the present Emperor, show that in the early period of his career, when everything succeded to which he put his hand, his system was the very contrary of what, afterwards, it became. In England, where power and influence are in the hands of the few, they retain it, by, from time to time, compromising with the many, and nobody doubts that without it, the question between the parties would have to be settled by main force. The Constitution of the United States was, in the strictest sense, a compromise, and unattainable on any other terms.

The Missouri Compromise was repealed in 1854, and agitation redoubled its violence. The so-called compromise with South Carolina, in 1833, was not a compromise, it was a surrender.

Moderation is with us, who, in our career hitherto, have little consulted the opinion of others, more than a duty. We, for the first time since the achievement of our independence, bend to the judgment of foreign nations. With France and England, who have armed in jealousy of one another; who are ready for war, and in a state of preparation for naval hostilities, on a scale of unprecedented magnitude, any untoward event, such as we have seen in the Mason and Slidell difficulty—and, when blows are exchanging, and belligerent and neutral rights in constant quest'on, another might occur at any moment—would serve as an excuse for intervention in our affairs. And what would, more than anything, in the eyes of Europe strengthen their position, and weaken ours, would be the fact of our carrying on our war, in a manner unusual among civilized nations; unaccompanied with offers of peace, and insisting on unconditional submission. The sensibilities of the world, when they desire to be shocked, are easily aroused. Rage against rebellious subjects, has been thought inhuman, when the people of Poland and Hungary were threatened with it by despotic and offended masters; but in the case of a difference among one another of citizens of a Republic, dating its recent existence from a successful revolt, there is an air about it which has already been the subject of criticism among those trans-Atlantic nations, which, Mr. Seward must have satisfied himself, when he surrendered the passengers by the Trent, are masters of the game, whenever they choose to come in.

And are they not masters of it? Are we not at the mercy of foreign countries? Is it not in their power, by intervention in favor of the South, to settle our fate, and sink us? And why should they not intervene, to-morrow, to-day, at any moment? Doubtless they would prefer to find reasons for it, answering, as they do, to one another, at the bar of the world; but those are not always waited for, as we see in many instances, our own, among the rest. Our independence having been declared only nineteen months before, on the 6th of February, 1778, our excellent, and never to be forgotten friend, Louis XVI., not pausing upon a recognition, or to raise a blockade, or for any minor object, entered with our provisional government, at once, upon a treaty of alliance, offensive and defensive, which was followed, soon after, by a French fleet and army sent to our aid, there being for intervention no better reason than a desire to damage Great Britain. Nor can we have already forgotten our recent treatment of Mexico, in the case of Texas. Nations do not love one another; and we, who have added rough manners to conduct not always satisfactory, must not expect to be dealt with from the point of justice and morality.

We must bear also in mind the natural desire of aristocratically ruled countries, to witness the failure of our institutions. The sentiment of sympathy, in the United States, was loud and universal, when, in the eventful year of 1848, crowns seemed to be falling off the heads of the monarchs of Europe; and shall they not rejoice, though too well bred to say so, when, in 1862, the Republic, whose prosperous career was daily encouragement to those domestic discontents, which are their main affliction, seems crumbling to the ground? The true mode, and the only one, of considering the question of intervention, is recalling what so often has happened in the history of nations, to assure ourselves that when it becomes decidedly the interest of any foreign country to interpose between us and the South, the interposition will speedily follow.

But they say to you, shall we treat with traitors? Shall we deal with rebellion as if it were virtue? If the question lay between parties who could refer their difference to a

court of justice, the reasoning might be good, but we talk
of nations. We cannot punish a whole people : even Nero
professed himself unable to do that. ·Certainly, the safest
and best rule, as well for communities, as for individuals,
is obedience to the laws ; but the idea of dealing with rebellious millions as we would with a bad citizen is inadmis-
sible. In the days when there were no *people*, rebellion,
which was an affair of the chiefs only, could sometimes be
"crushed out ;" but now the masses play their part, and to
speak of millions of rebels and millions of traitors is a political misnomer. When in 1776, to start on that brilliant
career, now eclipsed, perhaps forever, we shook off the
British allegiance and declared our independence, George
III. regarded us in no other light than that of rebels and
traitors. But he did not so treat us, though he hated us
most thoroughly.

Practically, it matters not how unnatural the rebellion,
how just the cause of the North, how indefensible the
course of the South, for the question must be regarded from
quite another platform; the concession, namely, that the
South maintain what they believe to be their rights. We
take up the argument on false principles when we take it
up in anger, and make it turn on the South being wrong.
The question is not, whether they are right, but whether
they believe they are right, and are in earnest. Anger may
be very well in the field, when the enemy is before us, but
an angry government is an absurdity. Secession is a mala-
dy, which has affected Northern Churches, as well as Southern States ; the Society of Friends, the Presbyterians, and
other religious denominations, have had their divisions, but
what is called their New School, though schismatic, is
sincere. If Mr. Jefferson Davis, in his inaugural speech at
Richmond, appeals to God, to protect and bless the people
who chose him to rule over them, shall Mr. Lincoln, after
his own speech of 1848, in vindication of the right of insurrection, to which I will presently refer you, say he is not

sincere? The Right Reverend head of the diocese of Louisiana leads in the field, a body of troops, a crime to parallel which we must go back to medieval abominations; but does any man doubt his zeal? The women and children are, in the South, everywhere on fire with secession, are we to set it down as hypocrisy? Mr. Rives, a man of the highest character, of the most conservative views, and opposed, on strong conviction, to the secession movement, is a member of the Confederate Government; is he acting unwillingly? The South, like the North, is full of citizens, sound in thinking, and pure of life, and they all unite in sustaining their government. They do not struggle against but enthusiastically support it.

How much out of the question it may be, that those who enjoy high places in the South, could be induced to listen to terms, the President and Cabinet can judge; but whoever will read the note of the 14th August, 1861,* of the Southern Commissioners, at London, to Earl Russell, in which those gentlemen, late the extreme advocates of slavery, reverently approach what they call " the anti- "slavery sentiment, so universally prevalent in England," " that high, philanthropic consideration, which undoubtedly " beats in the hearts of so many in England," can come to no other conclusion, than that the Southern statesmen, to conciliate an *enemy*, will pass through the eye of a needle. If the Southern masses can read that letter, by which they are made to knock under to the base bigotry of Exeter Hall, to the prejudices of the most inveterate foe of their institutions, to deprecate his haughty dislike, and, having sued in vain to one that never would touch but to ruin them, can refuse terms of restoration to this Union, which is theirs as much as ours, and which, alone can protect their negro property, the fury of civil war must have blinded them indeed. It is not to be credited that the peo-

*See it, as lately published in all the newspapers.

ple of the South—I speak not of those who think they have
founded an Empire; leaders pledged by ambition, and
oaths of office, to perpetual separation from the North, but
the population generally—should prefer to shiver in the
blast of the "anti-slavery sentiment, so universally preva-
"lent in England," rather than be reconciled to their own
countrymen. Is it possible that the citizens of the South
know what, already, they have come to—that their representatives wait, in English anti-chambers, to palliate their
sin by laying it on the North, that they, too, are for slavery?
Do they know that, at London, to propitiate the mighty
"genius of universal emancipation," it is represented, in their
behalf, as matter of reproach to us of the North, " that, after
" the battle Bull Run, both branches of the Congress, at
" Washington, passed resolutions, that the war is only waged
" to uphold that pro-slavery Constitution, and to enforce the
" laws, many of them pro-slavery, and of one hundred and
" seventy-two votes in the lower house, they received all
" but two, and in the Senate all but one vote?" If they do
not, let them read this dispatch and be instructed.

Nothing could, better than this letter to the British
foreign Secretary, illustrate the fact, that no country, based
on negro slavery, as modern society is organized, can have
a safe, independent national existence; and how sensible
those persons are, on whom has been devolved the office
of providing for the fortunes of the seceding States, that
they have not within themselves the elements of nation-
ality; that the South, now little more than an aggre-
gation of farms, to become a nation, must be born
again; that to acquire that variety of articulation which
goes to the national composition and quality, their whole
frame of things must be renewed; that to retain their
property they must restore themselves to the colonial rela-
tion with some European power, or come back to this
Union.

In this paper, a study for every citizen of the South, the

folly of the secession movement developes itself at its first
diplomatic step, as does the weakness of our Northern position, in the diplomacy of Mr. Seward. The extreme
Southern leaders delighted to call themselves fire-eaters, but
what is eating fire to eating one's words and principles?
To the proud stomach, fire ought to be a less uncomfort-
able diet than that on which the South have put themselves. When, for the sake of slavery, they left the Union to
establish a slave republic, they did not reflect, in the haste
of their movement, that the prejudices of mankind would
not tolerate such an establishment; just as in counting
cotton as king, they missed the fact that a rich and weak
nation is the poorest of all nations, and that, if their cotton
were really necessary to the world, the world would come
and take it, as they would come and dig their soil if gold were
found under it. When we think of all this extravagance
of Southern error, when we think how the North cruelly
and long goaded them to it, and that it is mutual ruin;
ruin to us as much as to them; that this slavery was pro-
sperity to the North, and mischief, only to Southern
masters; that the territorial rights asked by the South,
though very well to quarrel about, were, to practical purposes, nothing, and in themselves, but fair and equal justice, and that, could we but have forborne family difference,
and a few years longer remained united, we might have,
"confident against a world in arms," shaken slavery and
freedom, both, in their faces;—when we think what we
ought to be, and see what we have come to, it is perfectly
heart-breaking !

Emancipation is a word which sounds to virtue, for who
can doubt that Slavery is a blight to any region in which it
is tolerated? But it means with us in the United States, to say
nothing of the Constitution and laws of the land, and the
rights of property, that four millions of negroes,
now slaves, should be freed and added to five hundred
thousand already free negroes that are among us, making

four million five hundred thousand emancipated Africans, to be taken up into the channels of circulation of a body now overloaded and oppressed from the inability to absorb the five hundred thousand. And, as no time or tonnage would suffice, supposing the enormous sum of money necessary to such a purpose provided, to transport a nation of negroes to foreign parts, one of two events must happen; these unhappy beings, as the inferior and degraded race, excluded from the career of life, will miserably decay, by slow degrees, in the course of ages of oppression, or be more suddenly, but not more inhumanly, butchered in a war of races.*

But fanaticism which will not compromise, does not reason; nor do they, in any just sense, who, for political objects, avail themselves of it. After the death of Mr. Clay, the emancipation party, made up of New England† bigots, and clouds of unscrupulous politicians of all parts of the country, which had of late made immense strides, obtain-

---

* Within the last few days, there have been discharged upon this town, a number, variously estimated at from three to seven hundred, of negro slaves, sent hither, it is said, from the head-quarters of Major General Nathaniel Banks of the Massachusetts militia, father of the famous expression, "Let the Union slide!" being trophies of his warfare in Virginia; some, from age, filth and infectious disease, fit only for the hospital; others, young and vigorous enough to depredate upon the community, till they can be lodged in the jails.

† But for their persistent intolerance, it is sooth to say, that the slavery question would have had its day and gone by, like all the rest, from the funding of the revolutionary debts, to the surrender of Mason and Slidell; and the country would now be at peace, for not a State of the Union, but the six furthest from the slaves and having the least to do with them, would have pressed the agitation. The same spirit of *persecution*, which in the history of New England manifested itself from its earliest colonial period, and fastened, from time to time, upon various objects has for the last twenty-five years been concentrated on the *South.* The people of New England possess many admirable qualities, and the citizens of Pennsylvania have a high respect for them, but to be divorced from Virginia to marry Massachusetts is not a change of condition which comes within their views.

ing possession of several of the State governments, and
advancing in political influence generally, put forward for
the lead of the opposition to the Democratic party; till then
controlled and kept within bounds by Mr. Clay. They
succeeded in getting it, and established themselves in
1854, for the first time, on what may be called a national
footing, by the election of Mr. Banks as the Speaker of the
House of Representatives, who was nominated and carried,
after a desperate struggle of several weeks of balloting, as
the avowed anti-slavery, abolition Candidate. It was from
the Speaker's chair, which was the prize in 1854, they went
forward to their full success in 1860.

And now, is it the cue of this controlling influence to restore
the country to quiet, to come to terms, and make peace with
the South, on the footing of the Constitution and the Union?
Is that the object with which they pursue the war? Does
the anti-slavery interest, the active principle which scatter-
ing before it the less energetic particles of Republicanism,
has turned to its uses Mr. Lincoln's government, notwithstanding the wishes and prayers of a great majority of the
votes which elevated him—do they want harmony? We
must be credulous to think so. Would not any reader
of the proceedings of Congress suppose that we were
engaged in foreign war; and that the design of the
government, without exposing themselves to the male-
dictions of the world, by proclaiming freedom to the slaves,
was to damage, as much as possible, the enemy, through
his vulnerable side—that of slavery? If he were shown the
provisions of the Constitution of the United States, and then
the acts of Congress and orders to officers in the field, on the
subject of negro slaves, how small, would he suppose, were
executive and legislative reverence for organic law? Could
he doubt—do any of us doubt—that the present Executive and Legislature of the United States, if not checked,
will come at last, to what many of them long for now, a
proclamation of universal emancipation? The simple truth

is that, of the men now uppermost no small number have so long and so cordially hated the government of the country, that they may be said to have hated the country itself; and under their present cry for the flag and the war, conceal a strong desire of deadly mischief.

Is there a test by which they can be judged, the diplomacy of Mr. Seward, the measures of Congress, the constant language of the members, the appointments to place, the tone of the press, which can be construed in any other way than that to turn loose the negro, and injure and insult his owner, is the policy of the administration? Is there the man who does not see that the course which has been pursued on the point where the whole South, slaveholding or not, are most sensitive, and on which they are unanimous, is not only disturbing and insulting, but is meant to be—even to the gentlemen representing the border slave States in the Senate and House, who ought, of all others, to be treated with the most reconciling forbearance. Under such influences, the position of the country is a perfect dilemma; we must have victory, for if the South conquer us, the Union never will be restored; yet each military success being an addition to the strength of the abolitionists, the cry of emancipation, which is disunion, is only the louder for it.

Restore the Union, and where would these real and pretended fanatics be? Would it not be the downfall forever of all the hopes of the party now in power; would not abolitionist be the most odious of epithets; would not Northern democratic and Southern votes be again united, no longer to be startled by the anti-slavery halloo, and is there one of them that could politically survive the return of the seceding States to the fold of the Constitution?

To be in favor of the Union is one thing, to be in favor of the Union and the Constitution is another. What these men want is to keep the Union and break up the Constitution; and in that sense they are all for the Union. That late respectable cut-throat, Mr. John Brown, was in favor of the

Union. The high-scented negro, whom the President in his message to Congress* at the opening of the present session, beckons over as Ambassador from Hayti, will be in favor of the Union; the extremest worshippers at the African altar, who, in their love for the black family, or their blind hate of certain portions of the white, counselled Mr. Lincoln to solicit this accession to the diplomatic corps, to elbow his way among Senators and Secretaries at drawing-rooms and levees, are all in favor of Union. But what Union?—a Union which no eye will see!

To bring back the South as territory, not States, or without their slaves, or crippled in their condition of equality, might comport with the designs of those *who drive Mr. Lincoln's machine*, but when we recollect in what light they have, from the beginning, regarded the now broken compact with slave-holders, it would be downright simplicity to suppose that any party, controlled by them, should desire a restoration of it on terms that are either fair or possible. Is it not intelligible that, rather than it should come back, they would say in their hearts *after us the deluge*, and let the country go forward on its road of revolution?

---

* "If any good reason exists why we should persevere longer in withholding our recognition of the independence and sovereignty of Hayti and Liberia, I am unable to discern it. Unwilling, however, to inaugurate a novel policy in regard to them without the approbation of Congress, I submit for your consideration the expediency of an appropriation for maintaining a Chargé d'Affaires near each of those States."—*Message of the President, 3d December,* 1861. Mr. Lincoln is said to be a well-meaning man, and perhaps is so, having in that, however, no advantage over nineteen-twentieths of his fellow-citizens; but is it conceivable that any but the most devilish spirit of disunion could have dictated to him, for it is not to be believed the malice was his own, such a suggestion at such a time: not only abhorrent to the interests and instincts of the slaveholding country, but of all the North too, that is not absolutely abolitionized; as disgusting to us in Pennsylvania, as to you. Mr. Lincoln desires, we are told, to avoid too close communion with the extreme emancipationists, but it doth not appear, and in such a proposal one may see the hand, in his message, of the silliest and worst of them.

But even as I write to you, the proof presents itself, and deduction ceases to be useful. We need no longer infer the project of the party; you have now in the vote of the House of Representatives of the 3d of March, on Mr. Holman's resolution, the authoritative admission that the object of the war is not "the restoration of the authority of the Constitution." In a House of one hundred and twelve members, on motion of Mr. Lovejoy, of Illinois, Mr. Holman's resolution, that it was the sense of the House, that the war was a war for, and not against the Union and the Constitution, was laid on the table by sixty votes to fifty-eight, only thirteen members of the Republian party voting against Mr. Lovejoy, and but a single Democrat voting with him. Here is more than could have been looked for *so soon ;* for you have a present avowal of what it might have been supposed would yet a little longer be denied by all but the thorough-paced abolitionists, who, to do them justice, never disguise anything. I give you the resolution, and the yeas and nays on it, with the politics of each voter affixed, as found in a Republican newspaper, of the fourth of this month, in the daily report of Congressional proceedings.

Mr. HOLMAN (Dem), of Indiana, offered a resolution declaring that, in the judgment of this House, the unfortunate civil war into which the Government of the United States has been forced by the treasonable attempt of Southern Secessionists to destroy the Union, should not be prosecuted for any other purpose than the restoration of the authority of the Constitution and welfare of the whole people of the United States, who are permanently involved in the preservation of our present form of government without modification or change.

Mr. LOVEJOY, (Rep.) of Illinois, moved to lay the resolution on the table. Carried—yeas 60, nays 58.

YEAS.—Aldrich, Rep. ; Alley, Rep. ; Arnold, Rep. : Ashley, Rep. ; Babbitt, Rep.; Baker, Rep.; Baxter. Rep.; Beaman, Rep.; Bingham, Rep.; Blair, Rep, Pa. Blake, Rep. : Buffinton, Rep. ; Burnham, Rep. ; Campbell, Rep. ; Chamberlain; Rep. ; Clark, Rep.; Colfax, Rep. ; Conkling, Fred. A. Rep. ; Conkling, R,. Rep.; Conway, Rep. ; Cravens, Dem. ; Cutler, Rep. : Davis, Rep. : Delano, Rep. : Duell, Rep. : Ely, Rep.; Fessenden, Rep. : Franchot, Rep. ; Frank Rep. ; Hooper, Rep. : Hutchins, Rep. ; Kellog, Rep, Mich. ; Lansing, Rep. : Loomis, Rep. : Lovejoy, Rep. ; McKnight, Rep. ; McPherson, Rep.; Mitchell; Rep. ; Moorhead, Rep. : Morrill, Rep, Me. ; Morrill, Rep, Vt. ; Patton, Rep. ; Pike, Rep.; Pomeroy, Rep.; Rice, Rep, Me.; Riddle, Rep.; Sargeant, Rep.: Sedgwick, Rep. ; Shanks, Rep. ; Stevens, Rep. ; Trowbridge, Rep. ; Van Wyck, Rep. ; Verree, Rep.; Wallace, Rep. ; Walton, Rep, Me. ; Wheeler, Rep. ; White, Rep,

33

Ind. ; Wilson, Republican; Windom, Republican; Worcester, Republican.
NAYS —Bailey, Dem. Pa.; Biddle, Dem.; Blair, U. Va.; Browne, U. R. I.;
Brown, U. Va.; Calvert, U.; Clements, U.; Cobb, Dem.; Corning, Dem.;
Cox, Dem.; Crisfield, U.; Crittenden, U.; Diven. Rep.; Dunlap, U.; Dunn,
Rep.; Goodwin. Rep.. Granger, Rep.; Hale. Rep.; Hall, U.; Harding, U.;
Harrison, U.; Holman, Dem.; Horton, Rep.; Johnson, Dem.; Kellogg,
Rep, Ill.; Knapp. Rep.; Law, Dom.; Lazear, Dem.; Leary, U.; Mallory, U.;
Maynard, U.; Menzies, U.; Nixon, Rep.; Noble, Dem.; Noell, Dem.;
Norton, Dem.; Nugent, Dem.; Odell, Dem.; Pendleton, Dem.; Perry, Dem.;
Richardson, D.; Robinson, Dem.; Rollins, U. Mo.; Sheffield. U.; Shellabarger, Rep.; Smith, Dem.; Steele, Dem, N. Y.; Stratton. Rep.; Thomas,
Rep. Mass.; Thomas, U. Md.; Trimble, Rep.; Vibbard. Dem.; Wadsworth,
U.; Webster, U.; Whaley, U.; Wickliffe, U.; Woodruffe, Dem.; Wright, U.

In the same paper of the 5th March, is the following paragraph:

In the House to-day, Mr. Low of Indiana, corrected his vote on Mr. HOLMAN's resolution, offered yesterday, declaring "that, in the judgment of the House, the war should not be prosecuted for any other purpose than to preserve the Constitution in its present form," so that there was a tie vote; but the Speaker announced that he voted in the affirmative, so that still tabled the resolution.

Thus it appears, called forth by Mr. Holman's motion a little prematurely for the Republican leaders—but the gates were forced open and the monster revealed—that they fight not to maintain the Union and the Constitution, but to make a revolution to destroy the Union, to cancel the Constitution, and in Mr. Lincoln's words of 1848, to "shake off the existing government and form a new one that suits them better." The question being presented in the simplest and most direct form of parliamentary test, that of a resolution of the House—a resolution, unclogged with foreign matter, unmixed with anything more questionable than the Constitution and Union,—the abolitionists, on a call of the yeas and nays, boldly decline to abide by the country and its existing institutions, and lay on the table "the restoration of the authority of the Union and welfare of the whole people of the United States." They vote them down—and the mass of their republican followers vote with them!

I will ask you now, to recur with me, as bearing upon the political justice of a settlement with the South, to some

4

points of party history, as well recent as more remote. I desire by them to recall to your recollection that it is emphatically to the hard and uncompromising course of the friends of Mr. Lincoln we have to attribute as its immediate cause our present unhappy condition; and that the dogma to which the people of the South betook themselves for refuge from the anti-slavery hurricane, has flourished in other States than the slave holding, and in other times than those of 1860-1.

What is by the Republicans reproachfully called the slave power had, as they truly insist, with the aid of the Northern Democrats, ruled the Union for the much more considerable portion of the period which elapsed from the first election of Mr. Jefferson to the recent elevation of Mr. Lincoln. Instinctively opposed to over-governing, they, upon the whole, ruled judiciously, the let-alone policy prevailing, and never interrupted by the coming in of the opposing party without damage to the country, through the forcing system. Nor was there anything in this that revolted Northern pride; they did not ask, nor seek, nor want what the South so much valued. They attended to their affairs at home, and any traveller who opened his eyes and looked at the shining face of the prosperous North, and then at the laggard South, must have recognized the wisdom of their choice. But with the disproportion between the two parts of the country as it grew, and with increasing national wealth and power as they advanced, came the desire of the anti-democratic part of the North to possess so considerable a prize as the administration of them; and with it the temptation to take for their allies that active and extreme faction which were fanatically bent upon the abolition of slavery. The abolitionists gave at once to the struggle a sectional character, of the most violent and unsparing kind, and backed it by the fiercest denunciation of negro bondage so that when the North called upon the South to surrender the reins of government, they accompanied it with a cry for their property. The South, would fain have kept power as long as they could, and have contended, like other men, for mastery when it did not belong to them. But as they well knew, their slave property could never be as safe as when the Union protected it, their opposition to Northern ascendancy, fairly insisted on, would not, nor is it easy to imagine why it should, have led them beyond the limits of Constitutional resistance; and it was a bitter insult, a grievous wrong and lamentable mistake, when, after long and violent anti-slavery agitation, the South conducting themselves no worse than would any injured and perplexed minority, the election of anti-slavery candidates for the Presidency and Vice-presidency, with an anti-slavery platform, inaugurated in November, 1860, the final triumph of the exclusive North.

The elevation of Mr. Lincoln and Mr. Hamlin, to the eyes of all that chose to see things as they were, and they included the greater number of those who had cast their ballots against the Republican candidates, could not but cause a political crisis; which they flattered themselves would bring with it nothing more serious than a convention of the slave-holding States, to be followed, they hoped, by some arrangement, which if it did not deaden the fury of the anti-slavery agitation, at least would blunt its effects. But the preposterous example of South Carolina, bent upon at once withdrawing from the Union, and taking measures accordingly, led, in an evil hour, the people of Georgia, Alabama, Mississippi, Louisiana, Florida, Arkansas and Texas, to prepare for immediate secession, should it become, as they might deem, expedient; and upon the new President depended the course of action of each of these States.

Mr. Lincoln's advent to Washington was looked for with hope, unknown though he was, to the country, and deep anxiety; but it soon developed itself, in his addresses delivered by the way, that we were not to find in the Republican President, at a juncture that so much needed them, either the will, or the understanding of a statesman. Arrived at the centre of movement, he exercised no influence that was not negative, or more than belonged to inaction. He had, in one of his speeches on the road from Springfield, been reported as saying, with a levity now known to be characteristic, that he would *drive the machine as he found it:* and such seemed really to be the limit of his ambition. The whole session of Congress, before and after Mr. Lincoln's appearance, was a chaos of resolutions, and proposals of arrangements, by members from the middle States and Southern border, and mutual defiance of the extreme South and extreme North. But no State, South Carolina excepted, was irrational, for no other desired to leave the Union; not that there were not persons in the South, and members of the Southern delegations in Washington, who, like the Northern abolitionists, desired the worst, men blinded by passion, or ruled by the desire of change. But to be able to move, they must carry their States with them, and the Southern masses, like those of the North, were for the Union. The Union majority of Missouri was upwards of eighty thousand on a test vote; that of Virginia fifty-six thousand; Tennessee and North Carolina refused to stir, so did even Arkansas; in the Alabama Convention, the votes were for Secession sixty-one, against it thirty-nine; in Georgia so small was the popular majority for Secession, that a change of three or four hundred votes would have turned the scale. It was well understood that the adoption of the resolutions offered by Mr. Crittenden, and earnestly and solemnly pressed by him with all his weight of influence, would have left South Carolina to secede alone. If the President elect had but signified to his friends that their passage would be agreeable to him, the mischief would have stopped—the Union losing for the moment a single State. In Pennsylvania they would have been voted at the polls with no party opposition, for the politicians would not have ventured to contend with the current, so strongly did it set in. Nor is it credible that the masses anywhere, even in New England would have rejected them ; and petitions from the people poured into Washington, covered with names of those who had expended their time and thousands of their dollars to elect Mr. Lincoln, but now alarmed, and earnestly praying for measures of harmony.

We cannot bring back the past, but let us, for present instruction, bear in mind, that what the people wanted, the leaders refused because to save the country would have damaged themselves. The President was not yet installed, the patronage all undistributed, and to yield to the pressure from without and settle with the South, was to let down the pegs of every republican who had come to Washington as a place hunter, with no other merit than that of uncompromising hostility to slavery. The cry of the people for peace and union was so nearly universal, that the abolition influence seemed for a moment to quail, and nothing remained utterly unappeasable but the sacred thirst of the crowd that besieged the doors of the treasury. It is a melancholy truth, that if the crisis could have occurred after, instead of before the patronage had been distributed, there probably would have been a settlement and not a rupture ; for then, of a hundred politicians, the disappointed ninety-nine would have been sulky and silent, and the hundredth a place-holder and content.

Nothing was done ; the fourth of March came, South Carolina, Georgia, Alabama, Mississippi, Louisiana and Florida had left the Union ; and the border States had remained ; but the places—the places—those rewards of the faithful, which before, they were only looking for, they were now in the act of receiving, and the Government engrossed in giving. Future ages will with difculty believe that down to the 14th of April, the day after the Fall of Fort Sumter, no move was made by the new government towards saving us; but the message of the President, with the papers accompanying it, at the opening of the session of Congress, the 4th of July, 1861, are before the country, and put it beyond the possibility of doubt.* That Mr. Lincoln must have a cabinet to advise him is very certain; and, if they thought it necessary, the appointment of new representatives abroad, at the more important Courts, is intelligible; but that a government should have actually spent their time in emptying and filling little offices, of which it was of no sort of public moment whether the incumbent was of one party or the other, at such a juncture, is utterly inconceivable. It was the Greeks of the lower empire on the benches of the circus when the enemy was thundering at the gates.

Six precious weeks passed after the 4th of March, as the three months that preceded it, with nothing done to meet an exigency which it was in their power to control. The President says his "policy" was "time, discussion, and the ballot box." These were the measures of action, as denoted in the 4th of July message, †resolved on for the rescue of the Union! "Time, discussion, and the ballot-box!" They might be well enough for the States which had seceded, and useful in those that never would secede; but Virginia, North Carolina, Maryland, Tennessee, Kentucky, Missouri, where the Union men were in large majorities, but needed a helping hand and encouraging word; where events were precipitating themselves; which the se-

---

* It had nearly been much worse than doing nothing: the unanswered letters of the late Mr. Justice Campbell, of the Supreme Court of the United States, to Mr. Seward, dated Washington, the 13th and 30th of April, 1861, and published soon after in all the newspapers, are proofs too clear to be doubted, and it never has been doubted, that the Administration were on the very point of tamely surrendering Fort Sumter to the authorities of South Carolina !!!

† See the first two pages of the Message, for the President's exposition of his policy.

ceding States must carry with them or fail, and to which every seceding hand would apply a torch, was "time, discussion and the ballot-box," a policy for them? "Time, discussion and the ballot-box" meant the chapter of accidents. But soon Fort Sumter was fired upon and fell; the stars and stripes were hauled down, the rattlesnake hoisted in their stead; the indignant North started to their feet, and Mr. Lincoln had his cue, and a "policy!" It was a fitting prelude to the Mason and Slidell dilemma. There the Government waited and were swept into disgraceful peace; here they waited and were swept into uncompromising war. Five States, of the six which went out before Mr. Lincoln's inauguration, and three of the four which went out after, have been lost to us because, while he could not make up his mind, the Abolitionists had made up theirs to rid the Union of the slave States.

Thus, out of the extreme purposes of some of the Southern leaders, the greediness of the seekers of office, the malignant violence of the Abolitionists, and the miserable weakness of the President, came the final event of actual secession.

But the ground was laid for it long ago, and not in the South alone. Secession was the plague of confederacies long before America was discovered; and since these colonies were planted, under different forms, but always in the same substance of defiance of federal authority, secession has abounded, in every part of the country. Let me cultivate your feeling of charitable compromise by recalling to your recollection some of the facts. It was British arms, more than the articles of confederation, that kept us together during the war of the revolution, when the requisitions of Congress, so weak was its authority, the exigency being at its highest, were disobeyed by nearly every State of the thirteen.* The Federal Government was hardly or-

---

* New York and Pennsylvania are said to have been the two exceptions.

ganized, under the administration of Washington, when the New England delegations in Congress announced that, if the revolutionary debts of the States were not assumed by the Union, the New England States would secede. The very term, *secessionist*, was, no great while ago, it is to be believed, a favorite, for the American Anti-Slavery Society, at its annual meeting, in May, 1844, adopted a resolution "That secession from the present "United States is the duty of every Abolitionist."*

With the jealousy of the States of their sovereignty, of which it was neither wise nor possible to divest them, the framers of the Constitution dealt as well as they could, but always gently. It was a jealousy, of which Franklin complained, a century ago, which existed then, which went with us through the Revolution, and has adhered to us ever since. It was always, and is now, a necessary and honorable jealousy, arising from the love of freedom, and a just apprehension of power. But liberty has its excesses as well as despotism; it is easy to persuade men, however free, that they ought to be freer: and the office of inflaming the States against Federal authority, has been, amid the heats of party, undertaken by, sometimes, the most enlightened statesmen, and often, the meanest dem-

---

See a pamphlet published in 1845, by, or at the office of the "American "Anti-Slavery Society," with an "introduction," by Mr. Wendell Phillips, dated Boston, 15th January, 1845, which ends thus : "To continue this dis- "astrous alliance longer, is madness. The trial of fifty years, only proves "that it is impossible for free and slave States to unite on any terms, without "all becoming partners in the guilt, and responsible for the sin of slavery, "Why prolong the experiment ? Let every honest man join in the outcry of "the American Anti-Slavery Society, 'No union with slave-holders."

Boston, Jan. 15, 1845.   "WENDELL PHILLIPS."

The resolution entire, of the Anti-Slavery Society, was as follows :

"*Resolved,* That secesssion from the present United States Government, is "the duty of every Abolitionist, since no one can take office, or throw a vote "for another to hold office, under the United States Constitution, without vio- "lating his anti-slavery principles, and rendering himself an abettor of the "slaveholder in his sin."

agogues. Patrick Henry in Virginia, Mr. Yates and Mr. Lansing in New York, the distinguished men in all parts of the country who opposed the Constitution, the leaders of the large minorities of the Massachusetts and other conventions, which by majorities only, adopted it, the conventions of the States of Rhode Island and North Carolina, which, at first, wholly rejected it, mainly based their opposition upon the necessity of the States retaining their full power, as well as right, of sovereignty. Patrick Henry, to the position taken in argument, in the Virginia Convention, that the States, by the terms of the compact, would have the right, if oppressed by the Federal Government, to secede from the Union, answered, *True, we will have the right, but not the power.*

The Virginia and Kentucky resolutions, from the time when they were penned by Mr. Madison and Mr. Jefferson, and passed the Legislatures of those States in 1798—9, never ceased, in any part of the Union, to be the text of party, although from their doctrine to that of Secession, there is but a single and inevitable step. The Virginia resolutions declared it as the sense of that State " that, in case " of a deliberate, palpable and dangerous exercise of other " powers not granted by the said compact, *the States, who* " *are parties thereto, have the right and are in duty bound, to in-* " *terpose, for arresting the progress of the evil, and for maintain-* "*ing within their respective limits, the authorities, rights and liber-* "*ties, appertaining to them.*" Those of Kentucky, that " each " State acceded as a State, and is an integral party: that " *this government, created by this compact, was not made the ex-* " *clusive or final judge of the extent of the powers delegated to* " *itself,* since that would have made its discretion, and not " the Constitution, the measure of its powers, but that *as in* " *all other cases of compact among parties having no common* " *judge, each party has an equal right to judge for itself, as well of* " *infractions as of the mode and measure of redress.*" And further, " That the several States who formed that instrument,"
5

the Constitution of the United States, "being sovereign
" and independent, have the unquestionable right, to judge
" of the infraction; and, *that a nullification, by those sover-*
" *eignties, of all unauthorized acts, done under color of that in-*
" *strument, is the rightful remedy.*"

These resolutions, to speak of the work of such men as
Mr. Madison (who afterwards, in effect, recanted) and
Mr. Jefferson, in the mildest and most charitable sense,
were follies of the wise, for it is in the nature of government that the power of governing should be somewhere
lodged, and to denounce the perils of permitting it to be
exercised by the united discretion of all, and find for it no
safer depository than the uncontrolled pleasure of one, was
surely an impotent and unstatesmanlike conclusion.

They were the early fruit of Democratic discontent. But
in 1801 Mr. Adams and the Federalists went out, Mr. Jefferson and the Democrats came in, and the virtue of the
followers of Mr. Hamilton and Mr. Jay was next to be
tried, when in 1803 the purchase of Louisiana threatened
to swamp Federal influence forever, by bringing into the
Union and opening the great western country to a pioneer
population. The right of State resistance became now
New England doctrine, and was maintained by Puritanism
with hereditary energy. As a specimen of its tone, take
a speech in the House of Representatives, made the 14th
of January, 1811, after the Louisiana question had been
in fact settled for some years, and the subject long enough
before the public to allow the first effervescence of party to
subside, by Mr. Quincy, of Massachusetts, a member representing the city of Boston, and a gentleman of the highest
standing, on the bill to admit Louisiana into the Union.*
" I am compelled," said he, " to declare it as my deliberate
" opinion, that *if this bill passes, the bonds of the Union are vir-*
" *tually dissolved: that the States which compose it are free from*

* Gales & Seaton's Annals of Congress, vol. 3, p. 525, 11th Congress, 1810-11.

" *their moral obligations, and that as it will be the right of all, so*
" *it will be the duty of some, to prepare definitely for a separa-*
" *tion—amicably if they can, violently if they must.*"

But in June, 1812, when war was declared against Great
Britain, and their militia was required by the Federal government, by virtue of the clause of the Constitution author-
izing Congress to provide for calling them out to "repel
invasion," secession ripened fast in the cold climate of New
England. Governor Strong, of Massachusetts, backed by
a large majority of the legislature, proceeded under an opinion obtained by him from the highest Court of law of his
State, to carry into action the dogma of the Virginia and
Kentucky Resolutions, and refusing to furnish the Massachusetts troops, he set Congress at defiance. He put to the
court the following question, in an official communication
to them, dated Boston, August 1, 1812:

" 1. Whether the commanders-in-chief of the militia of
" the several States have a right to determine whether any
" of the exigencies contemplated by the Constitution of the
" *United States* exist, so as to require them to place the militia,
" or any part of it, in the service of the *United States*, at the
" request of the President, to be commanded by him, pur-
" suant to act of Congress."

To this the Judges, who were Mr. Chief Justice Par-
sons, a jurist of the highest standing, and a Federalist, as
were doubtless his brethren, Mr. Justice Sewall and Mr.
Justice Parker, of the straightest sect, officially answered
thus :

" It is the opinion of the undersigned, that this right is
" vested in the commanders-in-chief of the militia of the
" several States. The Federal Constitution provides that
" when either of these exigencies exist, the militia may be
" employed, pursuant to some act of Congress, in the ser-
" vice of the *United States ; but no power is given, either to the*
" *President or to the Congress, to determine that either of the*
" *said exigencies does in fact exist. As this power is* not dele-

"*gated to the United States by the Federal Constitution, nor pro-*
"*hibited by it to the States, it is reserved to the States respect-*
"*ively.*"

Governor Strong accordingly refused to obey the call for troops, but in his resistance, which did not here end, of Federal power, he went on his dangerous way, not supported by Massachusetts alone. Nothing but the peace of Ghent, signed in December, 1814, prevented that State, and perhaps others also, of the New England States, from withdrawing themselves,* in some form, from the Union. Sanction was to be given to this step by a convention which was to meet at Boston at the recommendation of the famous Hartford Convention, where the preliminary movements to that object had been organized, but all of which, including the assembling of the Boston Convention, became unnecessary, and fell through, when intelligence was received of the treaty of Ghent.

The original convention was called,† and sat at Hartford, Connecticut, in December, 1814, composed of delegates appointed by the constituted authorities of the States of Massachusetts, Connecticut, Rhode Island, and of delegates "chosen by local conventions," in the States of New Hampshire and Vermont, many of them men of the most eminent position, who after a session of three weeks, in which were fully considered the grievances of New England by reason of the war, agreed on, and transmitted to their

---

* It is but justice to say that between the secession measures insisted on during the war, by Massachusetts, which was the South Carolina of that day, and those of other States which assembled at Hartford, and consented also to go into the second Convention, there were material differences as to the lengths they ought to go, and the Legislature of Vermont declined to send delegates to the Convention at all, while the Executive Council of New Hampshire refused to call the Legislature to appoint them.

† History of the Hartford Convention, with a Review of the Policy of the United States Government, which led to the war of 1812, by Theodore Dwight Secretary of the Convention." New York and Boston : 1833.

several States, a series of resolutions, accompanied by a report, in which they hold this language :

" That *acts of Congress in violation of the Constitution are ab-*
" *solutely void, is an undeniable position.* It does not, however,
" consist with the respect and forbearance due from a *con-*
" *federate State* towards the general government, to fly to
" open resistance upon every infraction of the Constitution.
" The mode and the energy of the opposition should always
" conform to the nature of the violation, the intention of
" its authors, the extent of the injury inflicted, the determi-
" nation manifested to persist in it, and the danger of delay.
" But *in cases of deliberate, dangerous, and palpable infractions*
" *of the Constitution, affecting the sovereignty of a State and*
" *liberties of the people, it is not only the right, but the duty of*
" *such a State to interpose its authority for their protection, in*
" *the manner best calculated to secure that end. When emergen-*
" *cies occur which are either beyond the reach of the judicial tri-*
" *bunal, or too pressing to admit of the delay incident to their*
" *forms, States, which have no common umpire must be their own*
" *judges, and execute their own decisions.* It will be thus
" proper for the several States to await the ultimate dis-
" posal of the obnoxious measures recommended by *the*
" *Secretary of War or pending before Congress, and so use their*
" *power according to the character these measures shall finally*
" *assume, as effectually to protect their own sovereignty and the*
" *rights and liberties of their citizens.*"

Here was the doctrine acted upon by the seceding States in 1860 and 1861. Having pledged themselves to it, and to much more, the Convention, in adjourning, the 5th of January, 1815, resolved, by one of their resolutions, which were numerous and, at this day, read most strangely, in case their grievances should not be in the meanwhile redressed, that it was " expedient for the Legislatures of " the several States to appoint delegates to another Con- " vention, to meet at Boston, in the State of Massachusetts " on the third Thursday of June next, with " such pow-

" ers and instructions as the exigency of a crisis so momen-
" tous may require." Before that day the treaty with
Great Britain was signed, and the States which met at
Hartford, and such others as might have been represented
in the hotter region of Boston,* lost forever the glory of
anticipating the Secession of 1860.

The 24th of November, 1832, piloted by Mr. Calhoun
the State of South Carolina, by what they denominated a
nullifying ordinance, which was the new name they gave to
Secession, declared that "the several acts and parts of acts
of the Congress, especially those of the 28th May, 1828, and
14th July 1832, imposing duties on imports, were "unauthorized by the Constitution of the United States, and
violated the true meaning and intent thereof, and are null
and void, and no law."

When, in the session of Congress of 1836–7, the slavery
agitation, which it was hoped had ended with the Missouri
question of 1819–20, was resumed, never since to cease for
a moment, it produced among its results, state acts, defying

---

* The opinions, conduct and purposes of the Massachusetts leaders at that
day have gone into history in every shape. Mr. John Quincy Adams, said of
them in 1828, "That their object was, and had been for several years, a dis-
" solution of the Union, and the establishment of a separate confederation,
" he knew from unequivocal evidence, although not provable in a court of
" law; and that in case of a civil war, the aid of Great Britain to effect that
" purpose, would be as surely resorted to, as it would be indispensably neces-
" sary to the design."

The peculiar spitefulness of the opposition to the Union prevalent in that
part of the country, may be seen even better than in larger circumstances
in an advertisement in the Boston Gazette, of the 14th April, 1814, of the
Federal agent to receive subscriptions to the war loans, that the ' name of
" any applicant shall, at his request, be known only to the subscriber.'

The feeling of 1814, it will be remembered too, broke out again when Texas
came into the Union : and exhibited itself according to the newspapers in
resolutions of the Legislature of Massachusetts in the following words :—

" Resolved, That the annexation of Texas is, ipso facto, a dissolution of
" the Union.

" Resolved, That Texas being annexed, Massachusetts is out of the Union."

or seceding from a portion only, of the Federal Constitution. The rejected portion was the provision for the restoration of fugitives from labor, which, by the States enacting these laws, called Personal Liberty Bills, sometimes with open boldness, sometimes with evasive duplicity, was set at naught. These statutes engendered in malice, and not like the New England and South Carolina resistances of 1812 and 1832, in a sense of supposed injury, by which so many States set aside the part of the Constitution of the United States which they did not choose to comply with, had immense operation in the region at which they were aimed, in bringing and reconciling men's minds to the movement of 1860–61.

Massachusetts, in 1814, had not, by continuous action for a course of years, defied the laws of the Union ; Virginia and Kentucky, in 1798, had not approached, and South Carolina, in 1832, had not quite reached the point of action ; but here were resistance and defiance of Federal authority, violently, persistently, and, to all appearance, irrevocably adopted into state legislation ; and depriving, from time to time, citizens of the United States of property of a peculiar and most delicate kind, solemnly guaranteed to them by the Constitution. These enactments, repeated over the North, through the influence of the abolitionists, openly avowing their purpose to dissolve the Union, and of their party allies not only not joining in any desire to invade the peace of the country, but by a singular infatuation, to the last moment, refusing to believe it was in danger, were revolts against the Constitution in a more really dangerous form than any in which secession had yet appeared. They were more perilous than when secession took the form of opposition to revenue measures, or war, or to the alien and sedition laws, because aided by that irrepressible instinct of man's nature, which teaches him to love freedom and not slavery, they damaged, and were able to threaten the eventual destruction of an interest, at the same time the most vulnerable and the most wide spread, the very thought of a general assault upon which was frightful to all concerned in it. They were part of a system of torture, unrelentingly applied for a quarter of a century, by which the South were driven mad. The perplexity which haunted the owners of four millions of slaves, under the influence of incessant and ferocious anti-slavery agitation, from 1836 to 1861, that increased in violence and enlarged in extent from one Presidential canvass to another, was at last, too much for them, and in 1861, appealing from New England fanaticism, to the New England doctrine of 1814, that "States which have no common umpire, must be their own "judges, and execute their own decisions," slavery flew to arms from the Rio Grande to the Potomac.

The State that defies the Federal Constitution runs into revolution, and the reasoning that maintains it can do so constitutionally, is perverse; and so is the reasoning which insists that to annul one provision, by making laws against restoring slaves, is less unconstitutional than to annul them all, by going out of the Union. But the countenance given it by the organized action of so many States was not lost on individuals, and tempted to demagoguism occasionally, statesmen—oftener, less noble politicians. Mr. Lincoln's doctrine laid down as lately as 1848, as the rule of men's right to defy the government under which they live, is "inclination," and their power to carry it through. I quote from a speech made by him in the House of Representatives, the 12th January, 1848, on the former relations between Texas and the Mexican Union, of which it was once part. The speaker, who had voted that the war with Mexico was unnecessary and unconstitutional, is disputing a position taken, in the message of the President to Congress, touching the extent and limits of the Mexican territory. After saying that to ascertain the boundary between the two countries, it was necessary to know where jurisdiction was exercised, and asserting that

it had been fixed, not by treaty but revolution, he thus pro-
ceeds :

"Any people," said he, "anywhere, *being inclined, and*
"*having the power, have the right to rise up and shake off the*
"*existing government, and form a new one that suits them better.*
"This is a most valuable, a most sacred right—a right
"which, we hope and believe, is to liberate the world.
"*Nor is this right confined to cases in which the whole people of*
"*an existing government may choose to exercise it. Any portions*
"*of such people that can, may revolutionize, and make their*
"*own of so much of the territory as they inhabit.* More than
"this, a majority of any portion of such people may revo-
"lutionize, putting down a minority, intermingled with,
"or near about them, who may oppose their movements."*

Here is secession in its cups : from all this to the Virginia
and Kentucky resolutions, is the appeal from secession
drunk to secession sober. The authors of those resolves,
thinking with the rest of the world, that nothing but
intolerable wrong can justify revolution, find the way
through what they call an open door, but which was a
breach in the Constitution, to revolutionary defiance of it.
Mr. Lincoln deeming revolution virtue, "where being
inclined and having the power," the promoters of it "can
"shake off the existing government and form a new one
"that suits them better," disdains to mince into secession
this "most valuable and most sacred right" of rebellion.

And what does he mean, when, after telling us that this
most valuable right is not confined in the exercise of it to
"the whole people of an existing government," he goes on
to say that "any portion of such people that can, may revo-
"lutionize ;" and again, rising in the climax, "that more
"than this, a majority of any portion of such people may

---

* Congressional Globe, 1st session 30th Congress, Appendix, p. 94, where
the debates appear, the speeches corrected by the members who deliver them.
These remarks, therefore, of Mr. Lincoln, are from under his own hand.

" revolutionize ?" Does he mean that any fragment of a portion of a State may rebel and set up for itself; that in the ocean each drop is an ocean, and may declare itself an ocean, and have tides, tempests and sea monsters for itself? If they be " inclined and have the power," no part of the population can be too small to rebel ! ! !

It was the saying of the famous Carnot, a man of the first order, and an unquestionable democrat,—perhaps the truth lies between him and Mr. Lincoln,—after playing one of the busiest parts in the most effective revolution the world ever saw, that in his judgment it was better to submit to the worst government, than attempt to pull it down. But the tendency is to the denial of authority, and politicians stimulate it by false doctrine. In 1798 Mr. Jefferson and Mr. Madison dipped their hands in this kind of mistake ; in 1848 Mr. Lincoln jumps into a horse-pond of it. Who would have believed who listened (if there were listeners) to such stuff as this in 1848, that in 1861 the speaker of it would be sending his messages to Congress as President of the United States, and marshalling armies against doctrines which are unintelligible enough, but, when compared with his own muddy principles, are purity itself?

Ah! well would it have been for the country had this subject of resistance to constitutional authority, been always dealt with as it was by Mr. Clay, in the debate on the Compromise bill of 1850, when, in reply to a Senator, who assumed to sustain a friend who had thus erred, he said, " I know him personally, and have some respect for him. " But if he pronounced the sentiment attributed to him, of " raising the standard of disunion, and of resistance to the " common government, whatever he has been, if he follows " up that declaration by corresponding overt acts, he will " be a traitor, and I hope he will meet the fate of a traitor!"

But for schemes of resistance to authority, no brain too deep, none too shallow ; the stream of doctrine tolerating the Union, but denying its power, everywhere encouraged by political engineering, now soaking through the swamps of Carolina, now rushing over the rocks of New England, has swelled into the torrent of actual secession. We have nursed and petted what has grown to be a giant of mischief, and now, when he does his office, we can see nothing in it but "*causeless and unnatural rebellion.*" For exactly seventy years prior to the late Southern movement, this "causeless and unnatural rebellion" had rioted among us, in every part of the country, not only unpunished, but applauded and caressed, encouraged by the example of States, and countenanced by the precept of Mr. Lincoln!

Secession is no new heresy in the United States; and to the present hour, in the form of nullification, abounds in Northern statute books. Let Mr. Lincoln, whose lot is to make war on it, remember equal justice, and be ready with terms of gentle peace. Let him take down from the colors of the Union his vile scroll of *Unconditional Submission*, and write there *Conciliation and Compromise!* And would it be asking too much of a magistrate whom we made and can unmake; who was elected by voters and may be impeached by their representatives, to inform his constituents, the people of the United States, categorically and exactly, what are his terms of settlement? Is it a new thing that a free people should know what they fight for?

Such are some of the reasons—of which the number could easily be swelled—why it would seem to be humane, as well as wise and necessary, to come to an amicable adjustment, if possible, with the seceded States. But have the individuals who direct the present unhappy course of the policy of the country, reflected on the peculiarities of their own personal positions, when they thus push extreme measures to their utmost limits?

The government at Washington are servants of a people who have but one desire left, all others being absorbed in it, and should they disappoint them, let them look to the day of reckoning. Large majorities in the Houses of Congress unhesitatingly co-operate with them, and leave no shadow of irresponsibility, under which to take shelter. They have all the troops, all the money, all the legislation which the country can give. If they make good their promises ; if the war restore the Union, though coming to us with not a blade of grass, South or North ; if they possess us again of the territory of the United States, the mere area of land that belongs to us, we can begin again, and, profiting by our lesson, be what we had promised ourselves. But where will they be if they bear us to destruction?

Should the wild and desperate game, now playing, of Union and Emancipation, give us no Union, and only Emancipation, they will do well to remember that revolutions, which Barrere said *are not made with rose water*, when they come to a bad end, usually find in the leaders of them the first victims of a deluded and exasperated people. And let the Republican party, of whom the immense majority are citizens of moderate and patriotic sentiments, transporting themselves "beyond the ignorant present," put their houses in order against the day when revolution, in rags, may march up to the doors of every one of us. It is infinitely more probable now that eighteen months hence we shall be paying the last penalty of civil discord, than eighteen months ago it was, that we should be where we are to-day.

The people of the United States who have come to disaster under the delusion that, unlike the rest of mankind, they are immortal and invulnerable, in truth, have a quality not possessed in the same degree by any other population, the sentiment of individuality, the sense of each man of his own importance. This is infinitely unlike the very restricted estimate placed on himself by the inhabitant of other countries, where high rank, hereditary power, and old establishments, meet, in every direction, his eye, and with the aid of a government which quite relieves him of the

cares of State, let down his pride far below the point at
which is fixed that of the free and untrammelled citizen,
who, standing in a new and vast country, where yet there
are no monuments, looks round him and says, *there is nothing
better than myself.* This ought to be an element of strength,
though the converse exactly of the sentiment of the Roman
citizen, that he and all he had were the City's. Whether it
be nationally force or weakness, the people in the absolute-
ness of their will, could they reach this question, which
perplexes the present, and threatens their future, would
seize and settle it; but between it and them stand two organized governments.

The objects of that of the South are undisguised; it was
ordained for separation; to that their chiefs pledged themselves; they are in arms for it; to carry it through, and
prevent the restoration of the Constitution and laws, they
would use all means, ill or good, foreign aliance, auxilliary
troops, a return to European influence, if not dominion;
anything would be preferred to the Union; such is the
nature of their position. It would be impolitic to act on
the belief that the government at Richmond would listen
to any terms of agreement which the North could, would,
or ought to enter into.

But are there any terms to which the Government at
Washington would agree, which the South could, would,
or ought to enter into; to which any Northern Republican,
imagining himself for a moment a Southern citizen, would
consent? To which any people in arms, having risen to
" shake off the existing Government, and form a new one
" that suits them better," ever did consent? If the Government could to-morrow, bring back every seceded State
on the terms of the Crittenden resolutions, they would not
do it. And if the Crittenden arrangement be unadvisa-
ble, what other will they advise? There is none. And if
there be none, what is the difference between the two Governments, on the head of opposition to the Union? The

Southern victory at Bull Run strengthened the hands of Mr. Jefferson Davis, darkened the prospects of Union, and encouraged the hopes of European recognition. The Northern victory at Fort Donelson fortified the Abolition party in Congress. and enabling them to lay on the table of the House of Representatives Mr. Holman's resolution, that the war was for the Union and the Constitution, served as so much anti-slavery artillery to batter them both.

Our position is most critical, and demands all our energies. That governments must occasionally stand between the people and their immediate inclinations, is true ; but it is also true—and the administration ought to reflect on it —that the day has gone by when the people were not consulted ; when York and Lancaster could divide and deluge the land with blood, and count the people nothing ; that all they have they hold from us, and are to account for to us; and that we have no more stake in the game, playing between the abolition and secession factions as a game of dynasties, of ambition, of present power, and future Presidencies than if it lay between the White and Red Rose. We want peace and union with the South, not the humiliation of the South ; and the Government that uses us to seek for more, betrays us.

Is there, then, the vital energy in the people of the United States to hold their own, and stand firm against not one, but two governments, that are bent on their ruin ; not to be crushed to death in the conflict of organized and opposing forces, each ruling supreme in its section of country ; one insisting on unconditional submission, which is absurd, the other on perpetual separation which is ruin ; and both acting against the wishes of the people, and the Union of the States? Have we in the North fortitude to wait, undemoralized, for a Democratic House of Representatives, which cannot take their seats until December, 1863 ; as the passengers wait and cling to a shipwrecked vessel, and gaze

helplessly at sea and sky, tossed about by the tempest, so
many days more?

Are we already demoralized? The government is in the
possession of the political abolitionists, who fain would
perpetuate their power. They control the republicans, get
along, as well as they can, with the abolitionists proper,
and spurn the democrats as rebels. The state is deep in
corruption, and we its citizens, exhaust our pockets, empty
our veins, and peril our liberties in civil strife—which could
have been ended a year ago, without raising a man or ex-
pending a dollar—for the profit of political leaders, politicians, who availing themselves of the passiveness of some,
the thirst for office of others, and the fury of those of whom
John Brown was no exaggerated type, have in craft and
cold blood, through long years of treacherous agitation,
brought us to this pass, with no better apology for it, than
that they did not know what was coming!

They know it now; they knew it during the session of
1860--61. But the slavery question has, alas! its political'
mission—which is to make Presidents; and to settle it,
would extinguish too many lights. The political Abolitionists will do nothing for us—will permit nothing to be
done for us, and are as little to be trusted as the Abolitionists themselves. If we are to be rehabilitated, it must be,
under God, through our own energies.

But if we submit our necks to the yoke; if we yield to
unconstitutional pressure, to a mock reign of would-be
terror; if, by a system of spying and seizing, violations of
the person, violations of property, violations of the press,
violations of papers and private correspondence, we are to
be muzzled and hushed up; if the voice that is raised for
freedom and union is to be choked in men's throats; in
the North by Mr. Lincoln, in the South by Mr. Davis; if,
when our plainest word ought to be spoken in its loudest
tone, some Jack-in-office is to command silence; if, at an
hour when each citizen should be sentinel to the State, and

public judgment monitor to authority, we, whose blood and treasure support them, are to be kept under, like an Asiatic population, by a feeble Government, at the head of a numerous army, why then, God help us!

If that Almighty and beneficent Being to whom some of our pulpits* pray for success in the shock of battle, that we may make deeper gashes in our brothers' bosoms than they can make in ours, that our swords may be sharper than theirs, our artillery more crushing, would vouchsafe more humble supplications, to enlighten the understanding and change the heart of Mr. Lincoln, it is not too late yet to restore peace and Union. But until Providence shall listen to such prayers let us make up our minds to the worst, and looking at things as they are, see in them this, that *for measures having for their object the restoration of the Union, there could not be less chance than with the party now controlling the Federal government.*

Thus you have the views of the citizens of this midland region, who look to compromise with the South. It is the feeling of many of the Republicans, that an endeavor ought to be made to effect an amicable adjustment with the slave-holding States. That the Democratic party, which carried the State at the last election, and will sweep it at the next, will insist on an earnest and persistent effort, be it success-

---

* Is it not the bounden duty of the clergy, a duty to God and man, to do something towards extinguishing the flames of civil war? While there have been witnessed, within the year of our troubles, cases of ministers of religion who manifest the rancour of some of the New England pulpits of 1812, or those of England in 1650, they are, let us believe, rare instances, for the Christian Clergy comprise among them more virtue, learning and ability, than any other class. But much having been given them, much is expected of them; and their function, surely, is to resist, and not to be swept away by the errors of those whom they watch and should control. How could they so well do their duty to their country and their sacred calling as by an united movement? "I call," said the magnificent Chatham, when the question was to put an end to civil war, "upon that Right Reverend Bench, those holy ministers of the Gospel, and pious pastors of our church; I conjure them to join in the holy work, and vindicate the religion of their God!"

ful or unsuccessful, to restore the Union by measures of conciliation. you may be sure.

After more than a year of hostilities, with all the political complications. forced upon us from so many sources, and which now fill the place of the once fraternal relations between the two parts of the country, it is true that reconciliation must be difficult; but it is not impossible.

Men's passions may be high; civil war may have stirred the depths of mutual hate, yet national fury cannot blot out the sense of individual interest and safety. Nations even in the midst of a career of foreign conquest, rejoice to return to peace. Whatever the present state of the public mind in the two sections of country now arrayed against each other, if the people of the North and South could meet in a field, they would settle their differences. They would listen to the war speeches, and then make peace. Had the South known that war was to follow, secession would not have been resorted to. Had the North known secession was to be the consequence, they would not have tolerated the slavery agitation.

We are told that the South would not return to the Union;—never would consent to come again under the federal government—that the very children are inflamed with animosity against us;—but the difficulty is with the North, not the South.

The slave States, now out of the Union, seceded and betook themselves to arms, when they would have rejoiced to remain with us on terms which the mass of the Republican party desired to offer, and which now ought to be freely tendered them. Why should they not return on the same terms, on which they would have remained?

That the feeling in the seceded States is extreme, may be admitted; it is the natural and necessary consequence of the war, but it would be reasoning against the current of human motive to argue that the people of those States would rather suffer the ills which must accompany the

7

Northern attempt to subdue them, than to come to a fair and equal settlement, When did the weaker party—or any party—so act in national controversy? We are to suppose the men in the South are like the rest of the world, and will follow their interests—will accept the advantages and blessings of peace, if they can be obtained at no greater price than that of digesting their anger.

They have gone to war for what they think their rights, and separating from us is but the means, not the end. It is of hostilities, the declared, but not the only object. Nay, it was with the utmost reluctance that they admitted it within their line of objects at all. To give it the fullest prominence, it is but one of the purposes for which they fight. Now, peace may be honorable, and may be hailed and welcomed by all, though not carrying out the manifesto, which accompanied the declaration of war.

We went to war in 1812 in defence of our neutral rights. We were to the last degree provoked, as well as injured, and our determination, solemnly declared, was to require the abandonment by Great Britain, of the claim to exercise the maritime violences so long practiced by her, at the expense of our commerce. The war ended in a treaty satisfactory to ourselves, and honorable in the eyes of the world, by which we passed over without any mention whatever, all the objects for which we had been fighting by land and sea for between two and three years. The articles of peace said not one word about them.

The Government of the United States pledged themselves, formally, to maintain our right to the territory of Oregon to the parallel of 54° 40' of north latitude. Was the treaty dishonor, by which, to avoid a war, we accepted less favorable terms?

Washington—whose great name, like everything else that is American, must fall with the Union, and will come down from that of the founder of an Empire to that of the author of an unsuccessful experiment—Washington himself, by the treaty of 1794, yielded, for the sake of peace, a point on which the heart of the country was fixed.

The last march of European armies on the largest scale, was pointedly announced to have for its object the freedom of all Italy; but the powerful people who undertook so large a task paused, after a successful and victorious commencement of the war, and declaring their *programme had been too large*, made peace, obtaining the freedom of but a small part of Italy.

The South, too—it would be strange, indeed, were it otherwise—will make peace, if it be honorable and fair, not following their programme, and omitting disunion. The difficulty—I repeat—is not with the South, it is with the North. Doubtless there are other difficulties; the two governments, the government at Washington and the government at Richmond, with two entire national establishments, two debts, two armies, two navies, two allegiances, and all the infinite entanglements which have supervened since the session of Congress of 1860–1. But the main difficulty is with the North—the North ruled by the Abolitionists. While their dominion lasts, the difficulty is insuperable.

But should the next Congressional election leave the Administration in a lean minority, the Democratic party—if events do not in the mean time overwhelm the country*— will have it then in their power, and they will assuredly use it, to compel a change of measures: to require an earnest and sincere effort to bring about a settlement. Why should they not, out of their preponderance of votes, when

---

* As the *country* may be overwhelmed by the vices of a government conducted as is that of Mr. Lincoln, so may the *Administration* of it, and thus save the country. Why should not the accumulation of faults, and the enormity of their consequences, compel, at last, the President to that sort of sudden and complete change of a ruinous policy, and of the persons who influence it, which has been often resorted to—but usually too late—in other parts of the world?

opposed to the abolition party, in Missouri, Kentucky, Maryland, Western Virginia, Delaware, Pennsylvania, New Jersey, Indiana, Illinois, and California, with the aid of portions of the States of New York and Ohio, elect the majority of the members of the next House of Representatives? If they do, the back of abolition is broken, and the process of regeneration will be commenced.

You tell me—native and resident, as you are, of a slave State—that you are in favor of the Union despite the worst measures of which the government is capable. I rejoice to hear it, and find in such sentiments firm ground on which to build my hope. If other citizens of your part of the country be as true and patriotic as yourself, it remains only that the North do its duty at the polls to enable us to make our beginning, and break the fastenings which bind us to the fatal principles of the men now in power. When that shall be accomplished, we will apply ourselves to further effort; day will have begun to dawn, our hopes to assume form and shape ; the ship will be off the shore ; we can put sail on her and try the ocean. We will no longer be, as now we are, helpless. *To support the government* will no longer mean to stand mute when the Constitution is violated and the Union undermined.

To support the government will mean that we support lawful authority in lawful courses, and oppose it in all other. This war, in which we have been miserably involved—by the act of the South—by the faults of the North—we will support, as a war for the Union—which being assailed with the sword, must be maintained with the sword. We will carry it on, not with the power of arms alone, but essaying, also, the force of ample justice, and offers of frank conciliation.

www.ingramcontent.com/pod-product-compliance
Lightning Source LLC
Chambersburg PA
CBHW021526090426
42739CB00007B/796